IMAGES OF WALES

RHIWBINA

IMAGES OF WALES

RHIWBINA

KEN GRAHAM AND JIM TAVERNER

TEMPUS

Frontispiece: A detail from an Ordenance Survey map of 1875.

First published 2004

Tempus Publishing Limited
The Mill, Brimscombe Port,
Stroud, Gloucestershire, GL5 2QG
www.tempus-publishing.com

© Ken Graham and Jim Taverner, 2004

British Library Cataloguing in Publication Data.
A catalogue record for this book is available from the British Library.

ISBN 0 7524 3299 0

Typesetting and origination by Tempus Publishing Limited.
Printed in Great Britain.

Contents

Acknowledgements

We have been able to collect some 600 images and regret that there has not been enough space to include them all. Nevertheless we have retained them and they form a very valuable archive. We would like to thank the many people who have helped us and provided information and photographs. If anyone has been missed in this acknowledgement please accept our apologies for this oversight.

Other than those referred to in the text, the South Glamorgan Record Office has been particularly helpful in providing so much material on the garden village. We also acknowledge the help of Cardiff library, the National Museum of Wales and St Fagan's Museum, BBC Wales Archive, *Western Mail and Echo*, and Steve Dutton for the story of the Monico in his book, *Ribbon of Dreams*.

Mair Sims has been very generous in allowing us access to her collection of postcards and Vernon Llewellyn and Haydn Bartley are owed thanks as their photographs and information have been particularly helpful to us.

Others from whom we have had invaluable help include: John Revill, Alison Fear, Carl Gooch, Barbara Williams, Eithwen Jones, Mary Clark, John Hyland, Mary Drake (*née* Hyland), Ken Millward, Gordon Holton, Joyce Powell, Tessa Hughes, Andrew Davies, Commander Charles Scott-Fox, George Fox, Diana Lewis, Alicia Symondson, John Rhys, Alan Beynon, Eileen Thomas, David Salter, Judith Veysey, Denie Leech, Cliff Vincent, Val Yendle, Jim Yendle, Margaret Jones, Martin Smart, Peter Langham, Carolyn Saunders, Pentyrch Rugby Club, Nine Giants, Whitchurch Golf Club, Manor Parc, Margaret Slocombe, Jeff Heath, Phoebe Phillips, Clive Seddon, Ann Stanbury, Colin Pugh, Oliver Hyland, Denis Bartlet, Mary David, Frank Ronicle, Barbara Lowe, Carolyn Taylor, the Rhiwbina Amateur Theatrical Society, Heol Llanishen Primary School and Norah Woods.

The 'thanks for the memory' recollections of Edith David, Tom Lewis, Audrey Williams, G. Ryland and E. Walford were much appreciated in lending a personal touch to a sense of village life.

Editorial note: The variant spellings of the name of the village are used throughout this text and are consistent with the period they are describing.

Introduction

Writing in 1945, Edgar Chappell commented that 'the suburb of Rhiwbina is a development of the last thirty years. Until recently it was regarded as the area within the parish of Whitchurch, north of the Cardiff railway between the golf course and the eastern parish boundary'. Since the late 1960s it has been incorporated into the city of Cardiff; nevertheless Rhiwbina's endearing characteristics entitle it to be regarded as an urban village.

As seen from the 1875 ordnance map (p. 2), the landscape from which Rhiwbina emerged was for the most part agricultural, consisting of scattered farms and cottages, with Beulah Chapel, the Butcher's Arms, a corn mill and woollen factory all present, and with the Rhyd-waedlyd brook running through the middle. A truly rural scene! The first section of this collection of photographs attempts to reflect something of that scene.

The story of Beulah Chapel is an important one. Although it dates from 1849, it was recognised in a booklet produced by the church in connection with the centenary, that there was an absence of documents concerning its early history. Hopefully the photographs can tell something of the period.

The garden village story defines Rhiwbina's development and growth from the 1910s onwards. I hope that the photographs give a very interesting perspective on the origins of that important movement, the people involved in it and its status in the history of the garden village concept.

I am indebted to Edgar Leyshon Chappell, for his book *Old Whitchurch, The Story of a Glamorgan Parish*, the second edition of which was published in 1994. It is essential reading, giving a detailed study of this whole area, and I relied upon it heavily. I am also grateful to Wynford Davies for his booklet on Rhiwbina Garden Village. Both of these documents give essential background information to this collection of photographs.

For the chapter on local transport, I am grateful to Chris Taylor who has provided much of the information to support the photographic material and who lives in the garden village.

Chapter Eight reflects on some of the characters who have been part of the village story and the final chapter reminds us of the changes that have taken place as Rhiwbina continues to grow.

Liz, my wife, has been very supportive with helpful advice and preparation of the final draft and I am grateful to her as in all things.

I must acknowledge my thanks to Nigel Billingham (who has contributed similar collections on Ely) for encouraging me to embark on this venture, which has been a rewarding one.

I am particularly indebted to my collaborator in this project, Jim Taverner, without whose help I would have been greatly disadvantaged. Apart from his work in collecting images on computer, as one who has lived in Rhiwbina most of his life, he has been an invaluable source of information and encouragement.

No words of mine can express my appreciation to Beulah United Reformed Church who took the risk of inviting me, an Englishman, and a 'Geordie', to be their minister in 1980. This has been a rewarding and fulfilling time in my life and gave me, my wife and my family an opportunity to live in such a village as Rhiwbina. When I first came here it immediately struck me how people spoke affectionately of the 'village', and the sense of community and belonging it created. This collection is in no small measure my appreciation for this experience.

Urbanisation has, however, taken its toll as evidenced by the recent campaign to 'Keep Rhiwbina Alive'. Out-of-town shopping has taken so much away from the village centre. Hopefully the section containing photographs at the crossroads will evoke some memories, and will remind us of what we must work at to retain the unique characteristics of Rhiwbina. It is an obligation on all of us, local politicians, community leaders, business people, churches and residents, to work together to retain that unique characteristic which is Rhiwbina village.

In that respect we would like to dedicate this book to Alison Fear (*née* Cowley) who sadly died as it was being completed. Alison was born in Lon-y-dail and continued to live amongst us. She will be remembered with much affection for all that she contributed to the church and village.

Ken Graham
May 2004

one

Rural
Beginnings

Beulah Corner in 1903. This well-known photograph by W. Morgan Davies captures the rural beginnings of an area that was known then as *Rhyd Nant Walla* – the brook running alongside the chapel being known as Nant Walla. The lane continued up towards Rhiwbina Hill and the farm from which Rhiwbina took its name.

Hay making, probably in the late nineteenth century. This image evokes nostalgia of an age sadly long gone. In later years, this field was turned into a cricket pitch for the garden village cricket team.

Westwood, in Beulah Road (originally Deri Road), is one of the oldest houses in Rhiwbina, and dates back to 1855. The cottage adjoining Westwood, known as the Nook, is even older.

Village ladies prepare for a day out in their Charabanc outside 16 Lon-y-dail, the home of the Lewis family in 1923. Diana, Elisabeth (who may be the child in the photo) and Priscilla Lewis were all born in the upstairs room behind the tree. Alicia Lewis remembers the lamplighter climbing up his ladder in winter to light the gas lamp.

In this photograph, from left to right, are: Edith Robbins, Elsie Rogers, (legally adopted by Fred and Edith), Fred Robbins and May Loring, Edith's youngest sister. The family is known to have occupied Westwood from around 1910 onwards. Fred Robbins had much to do with the establishment of the Methodist chapel in Maes-y-deri.

Climbing up Rhubina Hill in 1920 then meant using this country lane. Today the M4 runs between the cottage on the left and the house in the distance, which can still be seen today.

Men at work on the crusher shed at Llewellyn's quarry (properly named Gelli Quarry). The quarry closed in 1934 as the Marquis of Bute would not grant an extension of the quarry area. Beulah church and many other buildings made use of stone from the quarry. Roman pottery, tiles and coins have been found from time to time on the quarry site.

The Llewellyns taking a break from work in the Rhiwbina quarry.

A horse and cart at the Llewellyn's quarry on Rhiwbeina Hill in the early 1900s.

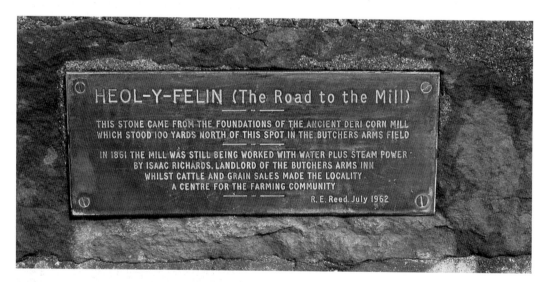

A bronze plaque set in a stone wall in Heol-y-felin is all that remains to commemorate the fact that some 100 yards north is the site of the ancient Deri Corn Mill, on the Butcher's Arms field, at the front of where All Saints church is now.

The likely origin of the mill was in the sixteenth or seventeenth century; the mill stream ran through the farmland of Ty Gwyn, north of the mill, to join the Deri brook.

During the nineteenth century, the duties of running the mill were combined with those of the landlord of the Butcher's Arms.

The Llewellyn family in the garden of Peacock Cottage on Rhiwbina hill. The cottage was the
home of David Llewellyn, the owner of Rhiwbeinor quarry – this is one of the many variants of the
name Rhiwbina. It was later the home of his son Llewellyn Llewellyn, and his grandsons Vernon and
Leonard. It was situated just below Woodhill, the home of the Corys, the well-known Cardiff coal
owners.

David Llewellyn, the owner of Rhiwbina quarry
and the grandfather of Vernon and Leonard
Llewellyn; the former still lives in Rhiwbina.

Mary 'Cwm Nofydd', an old resident of Rhiwbina, outside her cottage at the top end of the valley. 'Cwm Nofydd' refers to the location of her cottage; 'Cwm' is a valley, 'Nofydd' is the name of a stream. Sadly her cottage was demolished and has been replaced by an electricity pylon.

Mrs Criddle (the grandmother of Will Paynter the national secretary of the Nation Union of Miners, see chapter eight) outside her thatched cottage on Rhiwbina hill. Sadly, this is another thatched cottage that is no longer there.

Peace and Plenty, Rhiwbina Village.

Cattle grazing in the garden village. An early 1920s scene says it all about the rural origins of Rhiwbina with an abundance of cows and green fields. The scene also reflects a time of hope and optimism at the conclusion of the First World War.

A local young man in casual pose, his hat at a rakish angle, is captured on a summer's day on the Wenallt in 1908. The Wenallt has been and remains a popular place for rambles, picnics and family outings. Of special interest in the spring are the bluebells that cover the slopes in the wooded areas.

Rhiwbina Brook in 1927.

The Butcher's Arms in 1904. The two people on the right are the Butcher's Arms' landlord, George
Beames, and his wife.

   The girl on the wall is the mother of Haydn Bartley who donated this picture. Second left is
Haydn's grandmother, Mrs Wilde; she was the wife of George Colston Wilde whose father was
involved in the construction of the Colston Hall in Bristol.

   In 1861, Isaac Richards who was the landlord at the time, applied for a wine and spirit licence.
One of the grounds for the application was based on business at the Deri Mill, also operated by Isaac
Richards, and the popularity of local chapels!

William Smart at the gate of what was to become Smart's Tea Gardens and then Smart's Garage.

One villager recalls: 'what fun we had there on the swings and looking at the animals – monkey, rabbits and birds. We used to go in through a turnstile for 1d and what beautiful gardens there were – all roses. The gardener was called 'old booty'; he used to say "bloody" which we all thought was terrible. We were frightened of him really.'

Heol-y-felin looking towards the Butcher's Arms, *c.* 1930. The gate at the end of the lane led through to where All Saints is now and the Deri Corn Mill just before.

Fred Trimmer came to Rhiwbina to work on the garden village as a gardener. In the 1920s he purchased this house and established a nursery. Fruit, vegetables and bedding plants were sold from their shop in Lon Fach. A small housing development in Clos Brynderi has replaced the Nursery. Barbara Trimmer recalls celebrating her twenty-first birthday at this house.

Four generations of Trimmers. Fred Trimmer is standing on the left with his son Ernie to his right. Fred's wife, an Indian lady who came with him to this country, is seated. Barbara Trimmer, Fred's daughter, is standing next to her grandmother.

The grand opening in 1890 of Lisadrone (the meaning of this name is unknown) built on behalf of the Cory's, the Cardiff shipping family. Kitchen maids, upstairs maids, gardeners, butlers and pantry maids are standing and cheering while a local band, especially hired for the occasion, play. Lisadrone remained in private ownership until 1966.

Lisadrone is now better known as the Nine Giants public house. Frank Cory apparently used to rear pheasants on what is now the car park!

A family group in the grounds of Manor Parc in the 1930s, before it became a hotel.

The opening of the first Rhiwbina scout hall in Heol-y-Bont. The foundation stones were laid in December 1928 by both Mrs Carmen Cory and by Sir Rhys Williams Bart, DSO of Miskin Manor who, with key in hand, performed the opening ceremony. The scouter, on the top left is 'Sarge' Philp, who founded the group and instigated the building of the scout hall. The minister to his right is the Revd Samuel Jones of Beulah.

Beulah Road, c. 1925. Looking East, we can see some of the distant trees which are still there today.

two

Beulah church

THE OLD CHAPEL.

Beulah

THE OLD CHAPEL.

A sketch of the original Beulah Chapel as it might have looked in 1850. The sketch was made by John Weston Thomas, the Welsh harp maker and late member of Beulah.

Members of the congregational cause held services in a number of farmhouses in South Wales, and Briwnant Farm is thought to be where the founder members of Beulah Chapel decided to rent a small dwelling house, previously used as a Smithy, at the princely sum of £4.10.0 per annum. The site of this house has now been incorporated in what is now known as Canolfan Beulah.

Sunday School took place in the mornings and Welsh preaching services were held in afternoons and evenings and on certain week nights.

Revd John James, later appointed pastor, preached the first sermon at the Beulah Chapel on Christmas Day 1848. In 1851, the members felt confident enough to embark on a building scheme and the site adjoining the cottage was purchased for a chapel and graveyard. The cost of the new building was £138.

WILLIAM DAVID

DAVID NICHOLAS   JOHN PHILLIPS

Early Beulah pioneers. In 1850, William David was appointed as one of the trustees of 'all that piece or parcel of ground lying and being near a certain brook called Nant rhyd Walter', on which the church was to be built. David Nicholas was the church treasurer until 1869, when John Phillips took over from him and remained as treasurer until his death in 1894. Mr Philips has been described as a pillar of the chapel for those twenty-five years, acting as deacon, precentor and Sunday school superintendant in addition to his treasuring duties.

It is believed that this was a photograph of the guests attending an early Beulah wedding, *c.* 1900.

Revd J. Lloyd James. In 1860 when the total membership was forty-nine, a call was extended to John Lloyd James who served as a pastor of Beulah for nine years. Apart from his writings, he became a well-known bard under the nom de plume Clwydwenfro. Mr Jones' ministerial income during those years amounted to no more the £22 per annum. During the same period, visiting preachers received between 1s and 5s, plus hospitality!

The new Beulah Chapel as it would have looked in 1891 when it opened. By 1888, the debts on the old chapel were cleared. The congregation continued to grow and it became apparent that the old chapel was not adequate for their needs. Consequently, in 1894, it was decided to build a new chapel, on land on the opposite side of the road. Building operations began in March 1890 and were completed in February 1891 at a cost of £1,240, the chapel opened at a special service, presided over by the minister Revd D.G. Rees. The church membership was then 112-strong, with a total congregation of about 200; Sunday school numbered 160 people.

It is interesting to note the occupations of the new trustees appointed at the time. For example, John Phillips was a farmer, Daniel Jones a tin doubler, Joseph Salmon a tin assorter and John Davies a platelayer.

Up to that time, services had been held in Welsh but the switch over from Welsh to English came about in the morning service of 1898. At first this was for an experimental period of three months, but in December of that year, the church decided to make the arrangement permanent.

Revd D. Gwernydd Rees, the highly respected pastor of Beulah from 1875 to 1917, during a critical period of the development of the church.

In 1901, after twenty-five years' service, Mr Rees was presented with an illuminated address. During this time he missed only two-and-a-half Sundays through illness, preached at over 1,500 services at Beulah and received 320 into membership. Revd Rees continued to reside in Rhiwbina after his retirement; he died in 1933.

Revd D.G. Rees shaking hands with his successor Revd Samuel Jones. Between them, their ministry covered some sixty years – from 1875–1940.

Beulah Diaconate in 1917.

The Milward family outside the caretaker's cottage, *c.* 1920. Bessie Milward is standing on the far left with her sons Stan, Ken (who kindly donated the photograph and still lives in Rhiwbina) and Les.

The old cottage was demolished and the chapel house built in 1879 along with a new vestry; the total cost was £193.

The family have had a long association with the chapel. Esther David, grandmother to the children in the photograph, was the chapel caretaker towards the end of the nineteenth century and the beginning of the twentieth. She died in 1930 and was the last person to be buried in the chapel graveyard. Bessie Milward took over as church caretaker and continued to serve the church for many years until she retired in the 1980s. She continues to live nearby in Beulah Road behind the post office. The Milward family's cottage was demolished in the mid-1930s, to allow the road to be widened in Pantbach Road.

The building to the left is the old chapel; the round window that can now be seen on the gable end of the new Canolfan looks out from what was the gallery of the chapel but is now the church kitchen.

Revd Samuel Jones, the minister of Beulah from 1919 to 1940.

In his book, Edgar Chappell describes Revd Samuel Jones as 'a man of great sincerity and tact always aimed to maintain peace within the church and good relations with the world outside'.

During his ministry, one major structural scheme took place in the chapel. An American organ had been introduced into church services in 1882 but in 1925, it was agreed that a pipe organ should be installed. Mr T. Alwyn Lloyd, the garden village architect was commissioned to prepare a scheme for the installation of an organ chamber and new vestries at a cost of £2,200.

Revd George Phillips, the minister of Beulah, seen here with church members on the occasion of the church's centenary.

Another group of church members, with the younger members at the back. Revd George Phillips has gathered the group to celebrate the centenary in 1949.

The cast of the one of the Beulah youth club annual shows, *c.* 1945. This scene will hold many good memories of an important time in Beulah's work with young people. In the back row wearing spectacles is Wilf Lee, a leader and church organist. An organ screen in Beulah shows the church's appreciation for his contribution to their music. In the front row wearing spectacles are Jim and Dot Horsburgh; the youth club was largely run by the young people themselves but they invited Jim and Dot to be leaders – supposedly to give their activities an air of respectability and so be granted trust from the church deacons at the time! Beulah has had a long tradition in its involvement in children's and youth work. Revd Elfed Jones encouraged the transfer of afternoon Sunday school to be part of the morning service. The success of this development is in large measure due to the leadership, dedication and skill of Lilian Oldfield-Davies a highly respected member of Beulah church.

Beulah youth club at the Valentine's Day dance, *c.* 1949. In the photograph, from left to right are, back row: Barbara Brown, Derek Randle, Shirley Hughes, Haydn Jones, Margaret Jenkins and Alun Jones (Margaret & Alun were later to marry); Front Row: Pat Richards and Frank Kinsey.

When he was a boy, Alun took organ lessons from Wilf Lee, the church organist at the time. Alun started playing for services as a teenager and is still playing today, some sixty years later.

The Beulah Rockets winning an Eisteddfod competition at Merthyr miners hall in 1957. From left to right are: Graham Parsonage, Stephen Grey, Rod Thomas, Clive Seddon and Mac Thomas.

Three of Beulah's ministors. From left to right: Revd Elfed Jones (1941-1946), Revd Clifford Thomas (1952-1958) and Revd Glyndwr Jones (1959-1979).

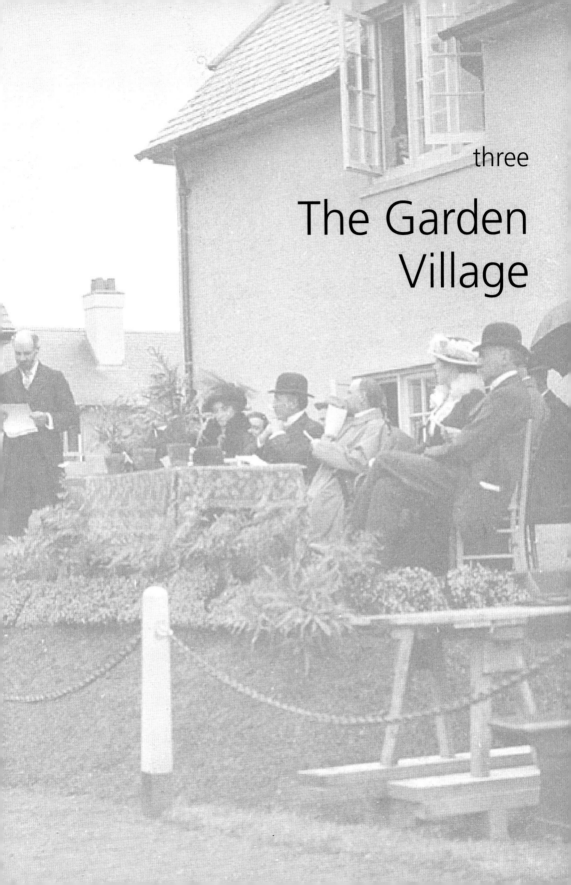

three

The Garden
Village

PROFESSOR. H. STANLEY JEVONS.
M.A., F.S.S.
HOUSING REFORMER
*Whose pioneer work led to the foundation of the
Rhiwbina Garden Village.*
· 1912 – 1914 ·

Professor H. Stanley Jevons, who held
the Chair of Economics at the University
College, Cardiff.

Professor Jevons resigned from his Chair
at the university in order to devote himself
to the task of organising reformed housing
schemes in South Wales. In particular
he became Chairman of the Housing
Reform Co. in 1911. The vision of
Stanley Jevons and other early reformers
was a 'series of beautiful garden suburbs
around Cardiff, each as well planned and
with houses as stately and suitable to their
surrounding as the beautiful park in the
middle of the town.'

Rhubina Field's brochure. Professor Jevons,
who lived at Woodhill in Rhiwbina had been
interested in questions of social reform for years.
A movement for reform was that of the Garden
City Movement, inspired by Ebenezer Howard.
In the 1890s and early 1900s, social reformers
were concerned with the appalling living
conditions which a number of poorer people
were subject to in Victorian society. Howard's
idea was to establish a company providing
decent living conditions for working people in
pleasant surroundings run on co-operative lines,
in which no resident was to own the house they
lived in. All residents would take out shares in
the company giving them a say in its affairs and
encouraging the idea of community
co-operation; a bold and radical concept from
which lessons could be learned for more recent
times.

RHUBINA FIELDS
CARDIFF WORKER'S CO-OPERATIVE
GARDEN VILLAGE SOCIETY
LIMITED.

"Health for the Child"

*Rail from Rhymney Station
Motor Bus from North Road.*

THE
Cardiff Workers' Co-operative Garden Village Society
LIMITED

Rejisterd Adres:—4 PARK PLACE, CARDIFF

ISYU OV
4,000 SHAIRZ OV £1 EECH
AND
£4,000 4½ PER SENT LOEN STOC

Chairman and Comity (pro. tem.)

D. LLEUFER THOMAS (Chairman)	F. STIBBS
CHARLES THOMPSON	LILIAN HOWELL
H. STANLEY JEVONS	EDWARD BLACK
J. CLATWORTHY	WILFRID J. HINTON (Secretary)

PROSPECTUS

The Sosiety haz purchast 10 aicers ov the Pentwyn Estate, Whitchurch, which liez immeedeaitly North ov the Cardiff Railway, between the Rhubina Road and the nyu Whitchurch Station. Boeth this staishun and Rhubina Halt actyualy abut on the estait, which iz, thairfor, moest eezaly acsesibl from Cardiff An impruuvment in the survis ov rail-motors, and speshal consesshuns tu memberz ov the sosiety in the wai of seezon and wurcmen's Ticets at speshaly redyuest raits, ar confidently ecspected. The cost ov the land is £200 per aicer, and the Sosiety haz the opshun for 18 munths ov acwiering a further area ov 20 aicers at £220 per aicer.

The Pentwyn Estate itself compriezes oever 100 aicers ov ecselent land, and the Housing Reform Company, Ltd., haz an opshun oever the hoel estait. For the moest part the land iz flat, but yet wel draind; and it wil be moest inecspensiv for bilding oeing tu the procsimity ov the railwai and ov a bricwurcs.

The hoel ov the Estate iz eezaly visibl from the railwai, and the Rhubina Halt iz mor yuesd than eny uther stoping plais on the lien, espeshaly bi holedai maicers proseeding tu the hils. Hens the enterpriez wil advurtiez itself, and but litl ecspens need be incurd in fiending tenants or capital.

The Sosiety wil erect conveenient and attractiv cotajes and housez ov from 5 tu 7 ruums, variing from £170 tu £250, intended for the yues ov wurcing men, scild artisans, clarcs, shop asistants, and uthers ov moderait incums. The rents wil probably rainj for the moest part from 6s. tu 8s. per weec, with perhaps a fyu at 10s. 6d. tu 12s. 6d. Including oepen spaisez, thair wil not be mor than 10 housez tu the aicer; and tenants wil be abl tu chuuz whether thai hav larj or smaul gardens. Urly applicants wil aulso be abl tu chuuz thair plots, and tu hav a vois in the desien ov the Hous.

On 6 January 1912, a society was formed to explore experimental developments in the spirit of the garden city movement; they operated under the title of Cardiff Workers' Co-operative Garden Village Society Ltd.

A number of sites were considered until eventually an area of 110 acres was identified to the north of Cardiff; known as the Pentwyn estate, it extended from Rhyd-y-walla at the village crossroads to Pentwyn farmhouse (now the Whitchurch golf club).

Builders, craftsmen and labourers engaged in the housing development assembled in Y Groes. The village scheme started with thirty-four houses: twenty-two three-bedroomed houses in Y Groes, and twelve larger houses with four bedrooms in Lon-y-dail. Edgar Chappell, in his book *Old Whitchurch* recalls visiting Rhiwbina with Professor Jevons for a simple ceremony of digging the first sod.

Opposite above: On a wet day in July 1913 after the first batch of houses had been completed, crowds gathered under umbrellas for the grand opening ceremony.

Opposite middle: The platform party at the inauguration ceremony. The Earl of Plymouth unveiled a sundial and a commemorative plaque on the facade of one of the houses with the initials C.W.C.S (Cardiff Workers Co-operative Society). Other speeches were delivered by Raymond Unwin, the Bishop of Llandaff and Sir Stafford Howard.

Opposite below: The ceremony took place outside Nos 6 and 7 Y Groes. One wonders who the child was peeping out of an upstairs bedroom watching Professor Jevons addressing the gathering.

New houses in Lon Isa in 1915. Building developments had continued in 1913 and 1914 with the society's second scheme comprising eighteen houses in Lon Isa.

Nos 21 and 23 Lon-y-dail just after their completion in 1913. In 1931, as the result of a great storm, the brook overflowed its banks and flooded fourteen houses. Several tenants had to be removed from their homes, and soon twenty-six houses lay vacant, eleven of them in Lon-y-dail where rents were the highest. The prospect looked grim at the time but the management committee acted swiftly, re-invented itself and by the mid-thirties the situation had recovered. Business prospered and vacancies were rare; there were now waiting lists for houses.

Lon-y-dail in the 1920s as seen from the railway with views of the Wenallt as a backdrop. Note the vacant space at the end of the road. Rhiwbina school would be built later on the site.

Lon-y-dail as the founder members may have imagined how it would look. A resident remembers: 'Lon-y-dail was a picture in the spring. Most of the houses had flowering cherries in their front gardens, and when these were in bloom, together with the vivid yellowy greens of the opening leaves of the young limes and planes, the avenue was a delight to behold.'

Homfray Road, Rhiwbina, Near Cardiff.

Pen-y-dre (formerly known as Homfray Road), *c.* 1919. Side-by-side with the society's own scheme, a further scheme of eighteen houses on the south side of Pen-y-dre had been carried out by Mr H. Avray Tipping. These houses were later acquired by the Rhiwbina Garden Village Society after the First World War with the assistance of the Welsh town planning and housing trust. Previously at the beginning of the war, the Housing Reform Co., started by Professor Jevons, had experienced financial difficulties and as a result was forced into liquidation. Professor Jevons had himself left Cardiff in November 1914 to take up a post as Professor of Economics in India. In pursuit of his dream to establish communities on garden-city lines in South Wales, he had lost a great deal of money.

The local site fortunately received support from the Welsh Town Planning and Housing Trust Ltd. After the First World War, building operations were resumed; with the aid of government loans and subsidies, further schemes in Pen-y-dre, Lon-y-dail, Lon Isa and Heol-y-deri were carried out. All loans and grants were repaid and 189 houses were now owned by the Rhiwbina Garden Village Society.

Ultimately the houses became privately owned when at a special meeting in September 1968 the tenant-shareholders were offered the leasehold of the house they occupied on very favourable terms. The results of this remarkable and pioneering movement remain today and as a consequence of its architectural and historic interest, this landmark site was granted conservation status in 1977.

Ramsey Macdonald, centre, (the Prime Minister in 1924 and from 1929 to 1935) is the important visitor to No. 16 Y Groes in 1920. On the left is J.D. Morgan and on the right Fred Stibbs. The visit indicates the importance that was attached to Rhiwbina Garden Village, as outlined in the aims of the Housing Reform Movement by early Labour reformers. While the original concept was to provide homes for the working classes in pleasant surroundings, many of the houses were rented by professional people and academics. Some referred to it as the Home of the Intelligentsia.

Committee members and friends of the garden village in 1913. Of particular interest is No. 1– Professor W.J. Gruffydd who held the chair of Celtic Studies at Cardiff and was not only a distinguished scholar but was also an astute businessman who was involved in the negotiations with the Welsh Town Planning and Housing Trust in 1915 and is also credited with providing names for the streets on the new estate. No. 2 is Professor Jevons, the leading spirit behind the move to establish what was to become Rhiwbina Garden Village. No. 6 is J.O. West of Hampstead who agreed to carry out the work on the first thirty-four houses by direct labour on a commission basis.

Also of interest is No. 4, Edgar Chappell, whose book *Old Whitchurch, The Story of a Glamorgan Parish* remains an important historical document and was recently republished in 1994 by Merton Priory Press. No. 5 is Fred Stibbs (South Wales Manager of the Ediswan Co.) who was Treasurer of the society and whose name appears on the original prospectus of the Cardiff Workers' Co-operative Garden Village Society in 1913, together with that of W.J. Gruffydd.

Garden village residents, *c*. 1920.

Ramsay McDonald on a visit to Rhiwbina on 15 March 1924 and seen here with residents in the garden of No. 25 Lon-y-dail. In the back row are: Edward Lewis, Mary Jenkins, -?-, Alwyn Lloyd, Mrs A. Lloyd, -?- ; In the centre row are: Mrs E. Lewis, Mrs Stibbs, J.P. Morgan, Ramsey Macdonald, -?-, Fred Stibbs, -?- ; and in the front row are: -?-, Phylis Stibbs, Elsie Stibbs, -?-. Well-known socialists lived here and were often visited by socialists of national fame. As a consequence, Rhiwbina Garden Village was often referred to as Little Moscow.

The garden village committee room, *c.* 1920. Here, residents paid their rent. During the Second World War, the room became an air-raid warden's post, full of stirrup pumps and buckets of sand and water to extinguish incendiary bombs. Fortunately no bombs fell on the village. This room continues to be known locally as the Wendy Hut and is still used by the Residents' Association and for other occasional meetings.

The management committee drew up regulations to ensure that the village remained attractive to live in and look at. Examples of these regulations included every tenant keeping the gardens, lawns, hedges and paths included in the tenancy in good order; people ensuring that garden refuse was not deposited on vacant land or open space on the estate; and tenants using reasonable discretion in the use of wireless sets, particularly during the summer months when doors and windows are open.

An aerial view of the village in the 1920s.

An important visitor must be at Nos 21 and 23 Lon Isa; this could have been the occasion of Ramsay MacDonald's visit.

This image of Pantbach Road in the 1930s shows the garden village's estate office. It eventually became the location for the public library and is now an aromatherapy clinic. In 1914 when the first batch of houses were completed, rents for three-bedroomed houses were 5s 9d to 8s 6d per week; for four-bedroomed houses £28 to £45 per annum. The society employed a staff of workmen including a carpenter, plumber, house decorator and other part-time staff, ensuring that the garden village was well cared for.

The pond adjacent to the eighteenth fairway at Whitchurch Golf Club in April 1942. The new Royal Ordnance Factory houses on Pen-y-dre can be seen in the background.

Newly built houses at the western end of Pen-y-dre at the beginning of the 1940s. These house were built to accommodate Royal Ordnance Factory workers who came to work at the factory site on Caerphilly Road.

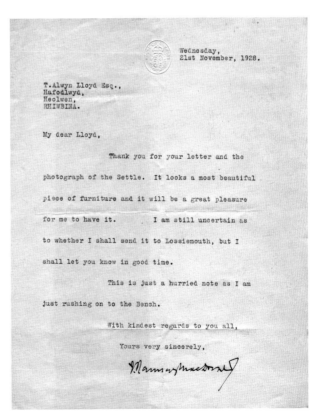

This letter, postmarked the House of Commons, is an interesting piece of memorabilia. It was sent from Ramsay McDonald to Alwyn Lloyd, the garden village architect.

A quiet scene in Pen-y-dre as the garden village continues to establish itself, in the 1930s.

Heol-y-deri stretching out towards the Wenallt around the 1930s. It is strange to see a lonely figure walking in the middle of the road. How different from today!

four

At The Crossroads

Beulah crossroads in the 1920s but still recognisable today. The bus on the left is believed to be one of Worrell's buses. The double-decker belonging to J.A. Rich is on the right and could be the Commer double-decker that was destroyed by fire in 1927.

Heol-y-Deri in 1918. Opposite was Duggan & James, demolished in the 1950s together with six bungalows; it was replaced by a block of shops, an unattractive modern development, which has now been improved with a pitched roof added to the flats above.

Originally two shops occupied the cabin: a shoe repairer and a newsagent. The cabin has since been redeveloped and is now a chiropractic clinic.

Beulah Road shops in the 1930s. W. Blow was an ironmonger, described as 'lean and bespectacled, whose stock was somewhat scanty consisted mostly of paraffin, screws, nails, and a few tools'. Charles Gooch took it over, and it is now occupied by a dry cleaner's. Next door was Jones the chemist, and next to that was Sylvester's.

Another view of Beulah Road looking west towards the crossroads.

Shopkeepers in Heol-y-Deri look anxiously at flooding caused by the brook overflowing after heavy rain, 1920s.

J.R. Jones the chemist in Beulah Road in the 1950s. Reg Jones had the chemist's shop in Rhiwbina for many years and was well known for prescriptions, potions and advice. Reg himself lived further along Beulah Road with his wife Eithwen.

Mr Gooch Snr in conversation with his son Peter at the door of their hardware store in Beulah Road. Charles Gooch started the business during the Second World War for the benefit of his sons Oswald, Bernard, Norman, Peter and Carl. Charles had previously opened shops in Whitchurch and on Caerphilly Road at the eastern end of Beulah Road.

The interior of Gooch's hardware store in Beulah Road. Mr and Mrs Gooch are on the right, Carl and Peter to the left. Apart from the contents in the store (just look at those prices) fireworks were on sale around the back. The shop windows were the only ones not blown out when a bomb dropped in Pantbach Road.

Inside Gooch's hardware store in the 1950s. Mr and Mrs Gooch are at the rear of the shop with Carl peering over the counter. In the foreground is a friend of theirs, Mr Craig. Today a dry cleaners occupies the premises.

Arthur Davies, the local newsagent. The shop was situated next to the HSBC bank of today. There have been many changes to the shops over the years. Some will remember Commerce House with its stock of drapery and haberdashery serving the village for over fifty years. The Co-op came to Rhiwbina in the 1950s, and is remembered for its catapult-like track arrangement for speeding the money to the cashier and back.

Beulah Road shops in 1936. The shops included: L. W. Tucker the grocer; Griffiths & Sutton Ltd, who dealt with electrical goods and stationery and who published this photograph on a postcard; Lewis the butchers, and H.C. Excell, a fruiter and fishmonger.

Dodingtons Stores on Beulah Corner in the 1960s (the site now occupied by the Principality Building Society). Dodingtons was taken over by Thomas & Evans in 1933. The manager, E. Walford, remembers some of the food prices in the days of pounds, shilling and pence, before decimilisation: eggs 1s per dozen; butter 1s 3d per lb; sausages 6d per lb; beef and pork 9d per lb; cheese 8d per lb.

A gloomy day at the crossroads in the early 1950s.

Mrs Wilson with Mrs Scott on the left at the counter of Wilson's Sweet Shop in the 1950s. The Wilsons retired from their shop to run an hotel in Llangranog. Their daughter Sue Chadwick still lives in Rhiwbina.

Smart's Brook Garage situated in Heol-y-deri at the rear of Beulah Chapel.

Rhyd Waedlyd culvert in 1961. The old library is the flat-roofed building next door to the newsagents, operated by the Nethercotts.

Another view of the work on the culvert at the crossroads in 1961, looking down Pen-y-dre. In the background are the cabin and, to the right, the building which in earlier days had housed the public library.

Another view of the construction of the culvert with Smart's Brook Garage in the background.

This view of Rhiwbina's crossroads in the 1950s was taken from above Jones the chemists in Beulah Road. The occasion was a fête parade. Note Whitchurch East's library in the background.

This view looks down Heol-y-deri towards the crossroads, c. 1930.

five

On The Move

This newspaper cutting is all that we have of a bus that came to a sad end in Heol-y-deri in January 1927. As the article explains, a petrol pipe broke and petrol ran down the gutter into a drain. Unfortunately a young lad dropped a match into the petrol and it flashed back to the bus. The bus is believed to be photographed at Rich's bus depot at the Philog.

John Rich had obtained a licence from Cardiff City and Rural District Council for a bus service from the city hall to Rhiwbina in 1920. In 1924 the service was extended to the Deri. The following years of his operation were fraught with competition from Cardiff City Council bus services. Finally, in 1927, Rich's buses were purchased by the city council for £12,000 plus £7,000 for the vehicles. All the employees were taken over with the business and the route soon became one of Cardiff's best earners.

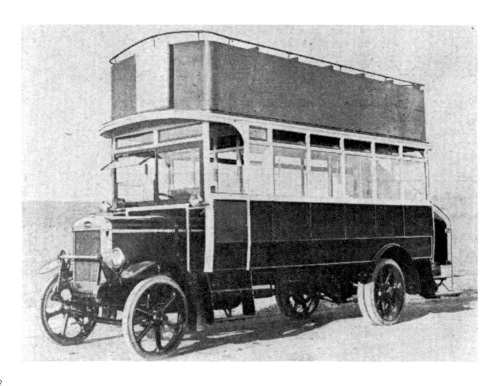

Above: From left to right, the buses include a Leyland from around 1920, 2 AEC's from 1924 and 1925, and a Morris from 1926. They are shown lined up in Kimberley Terrace in Llanishen on their last day of independent service in October 1926. John Worrel, one of the Worrel brothers, operated buses on the east side of Cardiff. After competition from the Cardiff corporation the service and vehicles were sold to the council for £1,250 including the four vehicles above.

The Worrel family came to Cardiff in the late 1890s from Norfolk. The brothers George and John started a business building cycles and eventually opened shops in many areas in South Wales in the 1900s.

A highly successful taxi service – Worrel's Taxi Cab Co. was also started; John's son Sydney began a bus service from Cardiff to Llanishen in 1914, when he was only eighteen, which was extended to Rhiwbina later that year. The service was transferred to John Worrel's name in 1919 and, with the help of William Smart (Cliff Smart's father), they kept the service going. For a time in the early 1920s, buses were garaged at No. 1 Beulah Road where John Worrel had purchased a shop. As the result of competition with Cardiff corporation, the decision to sell was made in 1926.

Opposite bottom: This advertisement from 1925 shows a double-decker omnibus, seating forty-six passengers and recently delivered to Rhiwbina bus service in South Wales. It was priced at £639 with Dunlop pneumatic tyres and at £595 with Dunlop solid tyres! If not the same, it is similar to the one that was burnt out.

Clarice Watkins, the milk lady, standing proudly by her brand new milk delivery van, the vehicle was purchased from F. N. Morgans in Beulah Road in 1936.

Opposite above: The bus pictured here is believed to be one belonging to John Worrel. William Smart is standing to the left of the coach. Trips were run from Cardiff to Rhiwbina for a pleasant day out with tea at Smart's tea gardens – a very popular venue in Heol-y-deri. Later the whole site became part of a garage and filling station. The area is now a small housing complex.

Opposite below: The No. NY 1520 bus negotiating a flood in Heol-y-deri in the 1920s. Rhiwbina's brook caused consistent flooding over the years until a culvert was constructed in the 1960s.

The garden village garage compound; we are left to ponder the circumstances that led to this elegantly dressed lady investigating the workings of a Riley car in the 1930s.

Lon Isa with two early cars. This scene contrasts sharply with the scene that meets us today in Lon Isa or any other street in the village.

At work on their cars in the garage compound in Lon Fach, *c.* 1928. These garages were demolished and replaced with concrete garages to increase the number available. We understand that the garages were built on land that was formerly designated as allotments.

Above left: William Smart, the founder of Smart's Garage, at the wheel of his taxi, in around 1920, but who is he waiting for? Notice the contrast with the horse-drawn vehicle in the background.

Above right: The Idris Evans bakery makes its last bread delivery in the 1960s in Pen-y-dre.

The shape of things to come? Fred Stibb's son Jack at the controls as he takes flight on the Glider Field in Llanishen.

Carl and Peter Gooch on the family Morris car in Beulah Road; the car had been decorated to celebrate the Silver Jubilee in 1935.

Ex-GWR 2-6-2T No. 5568 is seen approaching Rhiwbina Halt from the pedestrian crossing. The level crossing was discontinued, probably because of increased danger when diesels began to be used; they we a lot quieter than steam. Note the gas lamp; gas had been used until quite recently for lighting.

The Coryton Line.

The Cardiff railway was the last major double-track main line to be built in Britain until recently. Nearly a million pounds was spent on building a dozen miles of track which never saw the intensive service for which it was designed, thanks to the intransigence of the Taff Vale railway.

Cardiff railway decided to build its own route to Pontypridd and contracts were placed in 1898 for the first section to Tongwynlais, which is believed to have been completed in 1902. It wasn't until 1911 that Rhiwbina Halt was completed and the line opened for public service on 1 March. The name was altered to Rhiwbina in 1916. A 1921 timetable indicates the stations on the line: Cardiff, Heath, Rhiwbina, Whitchurch, Coryton, Tongywnlais, Glan-y-Llin, Nantgarw, Upper Boat and Rhyd-y-felin Halt.

The unprofitability of the section north of Coryton sadly led to its closure on 20 July 1931.

There were initially eleven trains each day on week days and five each way on Sundays; these were operated by steam rail cars. The existence of the line was of great significance to the garden village concept and its development.

One interesting recollection is that originally the name for Coryton Halt was to be Asylum! Fortunately the name was dropped. During the Second World War ambulance trains took wounded soldiers to Whitchurch station. From there they walked or were carried along St Margaret's Road to Whitchurch Hospital.

The Cardiff train leaves Rhiwbina on the down line in 1957. The footbridge is believed to have been assembled in the Whitchurch goods yard.

Home from work at Rhiwbina in the 1930s.

Petrol pumps outside Smart's Garage in Heol-y-deri in the 1940s with clearly displayed black market petrol. What, in Rhiwbina?

A petrol delivery at the forecourt of Smart's Garage in the 1940s.

An unbelievably quiet scene at the crossroads in 1953 with the No. 28 bus passing Beulah Chapel on its right. Buses used to turn around at the crossroads and head back up Beulah Road to Llanishen then on to Cardiff. The terminus was outside Jones the chemist.

The No. 22 corporation bus waiting at Deri Farm.

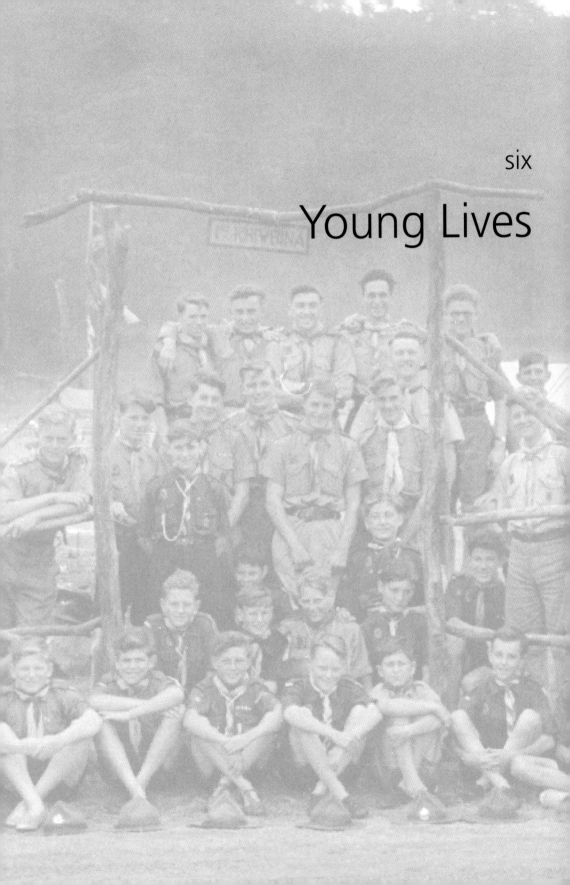

six

Young Lives

Phylis, Jack and Elsie Stibbs in 1907. Their father
Fred was a founding member of the Rhiwbina
Garden Village Society.

'Villagers of Tomorrow' at the village fête in the 1920s; the village fête was a special event
in early village life coinciding with May Day celebrations. Some of the new village houses
are under construction in the background.

Village children playing in April 1921; perhaps they are preparing for the May Day festival.

Rhiwbina school children's class photograph in 1927. Rhiwbina's first school met in the assembly rooms of the Beulah congregational church building where this photograph was taken. They transferred to the present school building when it opened in 1928.

Above: Enid Hamblin, the retiring May Queen, seen here with her attendants outside a bungalow in Heol-y-deri in 1926.

Left: A young boy proudly riding his tricycle in Y Groes in 1924.

This is the first photograph ever of the first Rhiwbina scout group in 1927. The scout seated far right in the front row is Jack Peterson, the Welsh boxer (see chapter eight).

Rhiwbina's guides and brownies, *c.* 1937. Photographed here with Brown Owl, Mrs Philp (wife of 'Sarge' who started the Rhiwbina scouts), they were taking part in the Empire-wide effort of all guides and brownies to raise funds to purchase two air ambulances and a lifeboat for the services.

Beulah's guides and brownies in 1939-40.

Rhiwbina infants school in 1936. From left to right are, back row: -?-, -?-, Eric Mitchie, Haydn Bartley, -?-, -?-, -?-, Alan Selwood, Robert Lewis and -?-; middle row: Laurence Meyer, Margaret Ridewood, -?-, Trevor Jenkins, -?-, Alan Edwards, -?-, Shirley Fields, -?-, -?-, Margaret Bull and Brian David; front Row: -?-, Joyce Williams, -?-, Beryl Williams, -?-, -?-, John Austin, Phillip Basset and Geoffrey Cooper; cross legged at the front: Jill Pollard, -?-, Dorothy McMillen and -?-.

Rhiwbina school in 1939. From left to right are, back row: -?-, -?-, -?-, -?-, 'Tubby' Jenks, Geoffrey Cooper and Allan Edwards; centre row: Maureen Phillips, Barbara Trimmer, Noreen Baker, Margaret Edwards, -?-, -?- and Betty Lee. In the front row, Jane Griffin is fourth from the right.

The Rhiwbina scouts in 1940.

A children's group, *c.* 1940.

Lt-Com. Davies seen here with the Rhiwbina scouts and sea scouts at Cardiff's East Dock. Lt-Com. Davies had organised this visit to the frigate of which he was captain during the Second World War; he too had been a Rhiwbina scout.

1st. Rhiwbina Scout Troop 1955

The 1st Rhiwbina scout troop near their headquarters, photographed at the junction of Heol-y-bont and Heol Caerhys in 1955. This splendid group reminds us of how scouting played an important role in the life of Rhiwbina. It is a sad reflection of today that it would be impossible to assemble such a group now! Donor Haydn Bartley and Diane Marjoram (later Haydn's wife) are seventh and eighth in from the left in the second row.

Opposite above: The Sunday school children pictured here raised money to help build the Rhiwbina Wesleyan Chapel in the 1920s. The photograph was taken in 1927 opposite the chapel site in Maes-y-deri.

Oppsite below: The 1st Rhiwbina scouts at the scout jamboree in Abergele in North Wales in 1949.

Ann Kynaston with her young attendants in Y Groes; she was about to be crowned the garden village May Queen during the fiftieth anniversary celebrations in 1962.

Rhiwbina schoolchildren in a class photograph from 1933.

Rhiwbina schoolchildren photographed with their headmaster Tom Pugsley in 1931.

The children of the garden village dancing around the maypole in 1962 during the garden village fiftieth anniversary celebrations.

In this photograph, a few people can be identified. The headmaster Mr Green is on the left at the rear; in the centre holding the ball is Jeff Robbins; in the front row, second from the left is Oliver Hyland and far right, Owen Saunders

St George's Day parade with the 1st Rhiwbina scouts, in around the 1950s.

seven

The Village At Play

Crowds gather in Y Groes for the opening of the May Day festival, an annual event in the life of the garden village.

The Labour origins to the garden village probably explain why May Day was set aside for special celebrations. The May Queen would be crowned on the village green in Y Groes and many residents would dress up; stalls and sideshows would add to the general festivities. There would be a resplendent Master Of Ceremonies with his lady, a town crier and the beadle. The following series of pictures are only a few from a larger body that give a flavour of those early May Day festivals. The festival idea was recreated in the 1980s and together with the 'Keep Rhiwbina Alive' campaign, it is to be hoped that the community spirit can be maintained.

The developing course of Whitchurch Golf Links in the late 1940s or early '50s. The houses on the left are in Pantmawr road joining houses on the right on Rhiwbina Hill. The Wenault can be seen in the background.

D. Jones and Alwyn LLoyd who played the part of the town crier at the 1921 festival.

The May Queen procession makes its way down Lon-y-dail for the May Day festival in 1928, ending in Y Groes.

A day of celebration as villagers in fancy dress gather for the May Day festival in 1922.

In fancy dress for the 1921 festival.

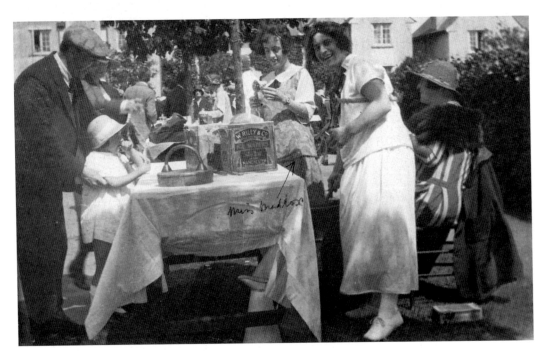

Miss Maddox and stall holders at the village fête in 1921.

Ladies serving on the drinks stall at the May Day festival.

Alicia Lewis (the daughter of Edward Lewis) is seen here being crowned the May Queen at the 1928 festival by the retiring Queen, Mary Williams. Among the young attendants are Alicia's sisters Diana, Elisabeth and Priscilla; Harold and Kay Watkins are to the left of the retiring Queen. The town crier is Alwyn Lloyd.

Rhiwbina's recreation club organised cricket matches as part of its programme in 1914. The portion of a field not immediately required for building purposes was secured for cricket. Cricket matches were successfully arranged with outside teams that year.

Team members of the Rhiwbina football club, Cardiff Cosmos, in 1919. A village resident, R. Barlow, remembers the team playing football in the field behind Lon-y-dail: 'We changed in the recreation club and washed our muddy bodies in a large stone bath with water, sometimes warm, from a boiler. Some players jumped in with their boots on and washed everything in one plunge.'

Rhiwbina's croquet club, around the 1920s. Ground had been obtained on rent from the housing society for the laying of the croquet green in 1914. The gentleman on the left is Fred Stibbs whose grandson John Hyland donated this photograph.

Members of the Rhiwbina croquet club in 1950. The ladies of the village spent many a happy afternoon playing croquet on the large green where the present car park is.

This photograph of village sports on the cricket field was taken by J.A. Hallam, the village's deputy architect, *c.* 1914.

Rhiwbina's bowlers in the 1930s.

Members of the Rhiwbina bowls club in 1953 are deep in thought; will it get near the jack?

Rhiwbina's bowlers' wives in 1951.

The Wenallt tennis club with Maureen Lee and Joyce Voden at the net. The club was situated at the rear of the Deri stores. During the Second World War the courts were taken over and used as a recreational facility for ROF workers in Caerphilly Road. The whole area has now been developed as Fairbrook Close.

Rhiwbina's tennis club in April 1953. From left to right are: Margaret Corrin, Joan Carter, Helly Schumann, Barbara Owen and Alison Cowley.

Rhiwbina RFC, the winners of the Fuller Cup in the season 1964/65. An advert had been placed in Rhiwbina's post office calling those interested to a meeting on Wednesday 14 February 1962 in the Memorial hall. As a result, Rhiwbina's rugby club was formed with Howard Saunders as its chairman, Joe Rees as its secretary and J.R. Jones as its treasurer.

Whitchurch Golf Club members are seen here in the 1930s with the old implement shed in the background, part of the original Pentwyn Farm. The back row includes: Charles Lewis, Reg Williams and Alf Berridge.

People are possibly gathered here for the opening of the Whitchurch Golf Club on 27 May 1915. During the summer evenings of 1912 and 1913, Mr H.T. Earl and lifelong friend Mr E.H. Targett were to be seen practising their golf strokes on the green fields of Pentwyn Farm. One evening they were spotted by Mr Sankey (a tenant of the farm and the uncle of the late Lord Sankey, the first socialist chancellor); suspecting that they might be in trouble, they were surprised to be given permission to continue their practice as long as they didn't hit any sheep! Golf chatter among businessmen using the Llandaff to Cardiff train led to the decision to form a small committee with a view to establishing a club in the district. Mr Albert Bullock agreed to act as the chairman with Mr Morgan Davies as secretary. These two, together with Messrs Earl, Targett and others, agreed to subscribe one guinea each towards the initial expenses.

After enquiries were made, it was discovered that the Rhiwbina Garden Village Society had given up an option that they held on Pentwyn Farm for building purposes. Negotiations led to Mr Sankey giving up his lease in August 1914 on the condition that he retain the farmhouse, outbuildings and orchard, together with grazing rights to the field surrounding the current second green. Fred Johns was engaged as a professional and commenced his duties in October 1914. Fred, together with H.J. Marjoram, the Radyr professional, were then largely responsible for laying out a nine-hole course which was opened in May 1915 with a match between the two pros.

In the early days, accommodation consisted of two corrugated iron and wooden huts, adjacent to the present seventeenth green. On the death of Mr Sankey, the farmhouse reverted to the club and plans were made for its renovation. In 1923, additional land was purchased from the Greenhill Estate enabling the further nine holes to be added, making it an eighteen-hole course. (This account is distilled from a longer account of the origins of Whitchurch Golf Club provided by Mr E.H. Targett, who described himself as the oldest original playing member in around 1938).

Women golfers prepare to take part in an open meeting on 27 May 1936.

Maypole dancing in Y Groes in July 1962 on the fiftieth anniversary of the garden village.

We believe that villagers have assembled for the opening of the recreation centre, *c.* 1921. Important figures in village life can be seen, for example J.D. Morgan, Edward Lewis, Fred Stibbs and Alwyn Lloyd.

Ready to drive off for the opening of the full 18 holes of Whitchurch Golf Links on the 24 June 1950. The gentleman, on the far left with hand in pocket, was the Club Professional, Fred Jones.

eight

On A Personal Note

Will Paynter, the national secretary of the Nation Union of Miners.

Up until he was eleven, Will Paynter lived with his mother and father in the small cottage at the foot of the drive leading up to Pentwyn Farm, now the Whitchurch golf clubhouse. Originally his grandfather had travelled from Bristol to be the bailiff at the farm. He died when relatively young, having been gored by a bull. To make a living, Will's mother did washing and ironing for the Pentwyn household. Will's father worked in the Cymmer colliery in Porth; each day he walked to the Taffs Well railway station, from which he took the train to work.

As a boy, Will recalls delivering evening newspapers, which he collected from the train at Coryton Halt. It was there that he saw train loads of wounded soldiers, still with the mud and blood of the trenches on them, being taken to Whitchurch hospital which had been turned into a military hospital at the beginning of the First World War. In October 1915, the family moved to Porth and from then on Will regarded himself as a son of the Rhondda.

Tom Lewis, better known as 'Copper Lewis', lived in Heol-y-deri. Tom came to Rhiwbina in 1935 and remained as the village policeman until his retirement in 1945. Tom was greatly respected and sometimes feared by local youth.

An old-fashioned constable, this recollection says much about him and his time:
'One very exciting occasion was the day Sir Stanley Baldwin was visiting the Earl of Plymouth at St Fagans and I was ordered there for special duty at twelve noon. About 9.30 a.m. I was polishing my uniform in my front room, which was used as an office, when I looked out and I saw a man passing; from previous enquiries he answered the description of a man seen in my district when a few houses were broken into. I put an old mac on, took my bike and followed at a distance. He went round the Brooklands and then into Lon Isa. He saw a lady leaving the house at the bottom of Lon Isa. He walked down on the opposite side and when he thought he was opposite, he crossed and went in the front gate. He walked to the side door. I watched him tap but fortunately the woman was upstairs with her baby. He opened the door and went in. I rushed in and caught him in the hallway. The woman standing at the top of the stairs holding her baby started screaming. I told her I was a policeman. A man neighbour rushed round and helped; he came back with my bike. As I reached Heol-y-deri, a resident Mr Idris Thomas was passing in a car. They stopped and asked me if I wanted help and they conveyed us to Whitchurch police station.'

In 1924, Tom became a Cardiff rugby player and was with the club for ten seasons, captaining the team in 1932 and 1933. Tom received national recognition when he was chosen to play for Wales.

On 4 July 2003 Edith David, who lives in Pen-y-dre, planted a tree outside the Rhiwbina library and on 5 July, she celebrated her 100th birthday.

Edith first came to Rhiwbina in 1924. In the early 1930s she opened Dyffryn Stores with Ethel Jones in Lon Fach. Edith remembers the friendly group of shopkeepers who organised charabanc trips to Tintern on autumn Saturdays. After 8.00 p.m., when all the village shops had closed, they headed off for Tintern, having a meal there before returning home at about 2.00 a.m. on Sunday morning – calling at various hostelries on the way.

A.T. Philp, known as 'Sarge', founded the first scout group in Rhiwbina. He was awarded the Medal of Merit by the scout movement and the MBE for services to youth. During the war, he was in charge of the Home Guard with the rank of Sergeant. He was also the surprised subject of a *This Is Your Life* television programme. Mr Philp ran an antique business in the Royal Arcade in Cardiff.

Sir Cyril Fox at home in his garden in Four Elms in Heol Wen in Rhiwbina.

Dr Fox, as he was then, came to Cardiff from Cambridge in 1925 to be keeper of the Department of Archaeology, and a lecturer at the University of Wales.

He was heavily engaged in organising and arranging the collection of 'Welsh Bygones' and took over from Dr Mortimer Wheeler in 1926 as director. He was knighted in the 1935 Honours List for his services as Director of the National Museum of Wales.

Cyril Fox came to Rhiwbina with his wife Olive and their two children when they purchased one of six properties which were built on land leased from the garden village trust in 1929 on a 999-year lease. The houses, described as being 'of Georgian proportions' were designed by Alwyn Lloyd for senior members of the museum staff including Professor Hyde.

The initials CFOF 1928 appeared over the door of Four Elms.

Sir Cyril's first wife, Olive, was drowned in a tragic swimming accident off the Gower coast in 1932, leaving him with two daughters. He later married Aileen, also an archaeologist, in 1933; he had three sons through his second marriage. Cyril and Aileen continued to live in Rhiwbina from 1933 to 1948 and when Sir Cyril retired they moved to Exeter. Their son Com. Charles Scott Fox recently published a biography of his father in 2002 under the title *Cyril Fox: Archaeologist Extraordinary*. Aileen Fox became a distinguished archaeologist and published her own memoir, *A Pioneering Archaeologist* in 2000.

Jack Jones in his eightieth year. Born in 1884 to a collier's family, Jack Jones lived in Rhiwbina for many years; he was known as something of a character and a great talker. *The Times'* obituary column described him as 'a personality to the end and delighted to be such' when he died in 1970.

He had been a miner and a miner's agent, a soldier in two wars, a trades union official, a book salesman, a parliamentary candidate, and a journalist, as well as navvying. It wasn't until 1927 when he was fifty, that during a period of unemployment he took to writing novels and plays. In the next twenty years he produced nine novels, three plays, three volumes of autobiography and a life of Lloyd George.

His novels include *Rhondda Roundabout*, about which Professor Gwyn Jones, writing in 1947, said 'in the chronicle novel or Valleys Saga, he stands alone; as the dramatist of industrial South Wales he has no serious rival'.

His novel *River Out of Eden* tells the story of the rise of Cardiff from the digging of the first Bute Dock to the year 1947.

Wynford Davies with his son Andrew in the late 1930s. Wynford compiled a history of Rhiwbina Garden Village which was published in 1985.

Andrew was educated at Rhiwbina school and Whitchurch grammar school. Through his writing for children, including *Conrad's War* and the Marmalade Atkins series, he has earned a number of awards, in particular the Guardian Children's Fiction Award.

He wrote the television series, *A Very Peculiar Practice* and has scripted many adaptations for television. They include: *To Serve Them All Our Days*, *House of Cards*, *Pride and Prejudice*, *Middlemarch*, *Vanity Fair*, *Daniel Deronda*, *Boudica* and *He Knew He Was Right*. Andrew also provided the screenplay for the film *Bridget Jones' Diary*.

JACK PETERSEN

Jack Peterson, born in 1911, is seen here during sparring practice. Jack won the amateur light-heavyweight crown in 1931 after which he turned professional. He held the British and Empire titles, which he successfully defended against Len Harvey in 1936. Jack was a scout with the 1st Rhiwbina scouts.

Rachel Thomas who came to live in Rhiwbina after her marriage to Hywel Thomas in 1932. She lived in Y Goedwig and remained in Rhiwbina until her death in 1995 at the age of ninety. Her birth and early life in Alltwen in the Swansea Valley was an important influence in her life.

In 1938 Rachel made her screen debut starring in the film *Proud Valley* with Paul Robeson. Rachel was a popular actress well known for her portrayal of the typical Welsh mother.

In 1960 she played the role of Mam in the BBC television production *How Green Was My Valley*. Her last screen role was as an old lady prepared to defend her farm with a shotgun in *Whistling Boy*.

Quiet and unassuming she was always willing to support Welsh and local charity events.

Alun Oldfield Davies had a distinguished career as controller of BBC Wales from 1948 to 1967. He was also Vice President of the Governing Body of St Fagans Folk Museum from 1967 to 1972. He lived for many years in Rhiwbina in the bungalow directly opposite the Monico. Alun's wife Lillian was a highly respected and much loved member and junior church leader in Beulah.

Selwyn Roderick joined BBC Wales in 1953 after working in radio in America. During his career as a TV producer, Selwyn worked on many outside broadcasts, the North Wales coverage of the Coronation being one as well as regional editions of *Come Dancing*. He has also worked on many documentaries including a two-month series on Patagonia in Welsh and English, which studied the history of Welsh settlements.

Selwyn also produced programmes in the initial series of *Your Life in Their Hands*, as well as coverage of the tenth and twentieth anniversaries of the conquest of Everest by Hilary and Tensing; some of their training having been undertaken on Snowdon.

Selwyn moved to Rhiwbina in the 1950s and has remained here ever since.

Iowerth Peate receiving a presentation on his retirement as the curator of St Fagans Folk Museum, in 1971.

Iowerth Peate joined the staff of the National Museum of Wales in 1927 and following the establishment of the Folk Museum at St Fagans he was appointed as keeper-in-charge in 1948 and curator in 1953. Apart from his work at St Fagans he published five volumes of poetry and two autobiographical works.

Iowerth lived in Rhiwbina Garden Village from the early 1930s and moved in 1948 to take up residence on the upper floor of St Fagan's Castle.

Catrin Stevens wrote of him that the gardens and castle of St Fagans are 'a tangible memorial to his vision and mission throughout his life'. She added: 'As the museum's prime mover, creator and first curator, Iowerth Peate remains synonymous with the reputation of perhaps our most internationally esteemed national institution.'

A young Andy Fairweather Lowe with his band Amen Corner in 1968. In the late 1960s they had a number one hit single with *(If Paradise is) Half as Nice*, following it up with another, *Bend Me Shake Me*. In the 1970s, Andy went solo and will be particularly remembered for his hit *Wide Eyed and Legless*. In recent years he has been associated with the Eric Clapton band. Andy and his wife Barbara came to live in Rhiwbina in 1970 and have remained here ever since.

Stan Stennett as well as being a Rhiwbina resident is a well-known Welsh comedian and accomplished musician, having learned to play the guitar when he was twelve years old.

After serving in the forces during the Second World War, Stan had his first break appearing with Sir Harry Secombe in *Welsh Rarebit*, a popular radio show. Stan later joined the Black and White Minstrel Show in the 1960s and has appeared in many theatres with well-known artistes in a successful career. Stan even came to our television screens appearing as the character Sid Hooper in *Crossroads*. Perhaps he will be best remembered for his work in pantomime, as he starred in over fifty of them and formed his own production company.

nine

The Village
Grows

A sketch of the new recreation hall by Mr T. Alwyn Lloyd, the village architect. The building was completed between 1921 and 1922. Four new tennis courts and a bowling green were to be ready for the forthcoming season.

After the establishment of the garden village, Rhiwbina developed rapidly in the 1930s and after the Second World War. Private housing began to eat up the space surrounding the crossroads and modern Rhiwbina began to emerge. These images from the 1930s are an indication of that process.

Wenallt Road leading north from the Deri was the scene of a tragic accident in September 1936. It seems that Maurice King, who was twenty-three, from Norfolk and Norwich Aero Club, flew a B.A. Eagle over Rhiwbina towards Wenallt Road with Mr H.B. Elwell, a resident of Wenallt Road, as a passenger. Mr Elwell, a member of the Cardiff Aeroplane Club, was seen waving from the back seat to his wife in their garden as they flew past. However the pilot lost control, the plane struck telephone wires, caught fire and no one survived. The account of an eye witness, Miss Wilson, at the Deri bus terminus was reported in the *South Wales Echo*: 'The machine flying very low came into sight from the direction of the Golf Links. It almost touched the roof of the Chalet Café and was swinging in a most extraordinary fashion. It crossed over towards the Wenallt and appeared to turn half a loop. Then it crashed in a corner of the field up the hill.'

The bowling green and pavilion, c. 1935

Countess Mountbatten inspecting the brownies of the 64th Cardiff (Rhiwbina) Pack after opening the memorial hall in Rhiwbina on 13 June 1968. The memorial hall is well used by many groups for social occasions and not least by Rhiwbina's amateur theatrical society, who stage their productions there.

All Saints church in Wales; the choir, seen here at the rear of the church in around 1935, include Norah Wood, aged sixteen, second from the right on the back row; Choir Master Walter Charles, fifth from the left on the first seated row; the two curates Revd David Griffiths and Revd Beynon and the lay reader David Hopkins.

As Rhiwbina continued to expand in the 1930s, new churches began to emerge. On the land adjacent to the site of the Deri Mill, All Saints church was dedicated by the Bishop in September 1931. The church was built by Watts and Gale at a cost of £1,080.

We are grateful to Howard Reeve who provided this photograph of his parents' wedding in the Methodist church in Rhiwbina in April 1938. Beatrice Aston, who was twenty-six at the time, was a Sunday school teacher at the church; Benjamin, a Baptist Minister, was sixty-two and had been widowed twice before. They had two children.

The Monico cinema as it would have been seen in the 1960s. The Splott (Cardiff) Cinema Co. opened the Monico cinema on 19 April 1937.

The façade of the Monico gradually deteriorated over the years and its ferro-concrete exterior was badly in need of repair. The city council provided a grant to enable the building to be clad in what has been described as a 'cast iron waistcoat'. It was also described as a 'corrugated iron warehouse'.

In the 1970s the Monico received another make-over when it was converted into two cinemas. The cinema was divided horizontally with its original stage being lifted 8ft in the main auditorium which still retained its screen size, whilst almost 250 tonnes of earth had to be removed from the ground floor to enable the installation of the smaller Monico two-screen.

In 1976, the cinema was sold to Rank who sold it to Brian Bull in 1977. The cinema is reputed to be the first privately owned cinema to have a Dolby stereo surround-sound within both its screens. It is also said to have been one of the first cinemas to have a Saturday morning club for children.

Sadly, in Augus 2003, crowds gathered to watch the demolition of the cinema as it had to yield to the advent of the multiplex cinemas in Cardiff. The familiar landmark disappeared from the Rhiwbina landscape to be replaced by a housing complex, which continues to carry the name Monico.

On a wet day members and friends gather on the site of the new Baptist church, for the turf-cutting ceremony. Bethany church was re-located from its building in St Mary Street in Cardiff to this new site in Heol Llanishen Fach. Part of the old chapel can still be seen inside Howell's store.

Opposite above: Mrs Nancy Andrews prepares to cut the turf at a special ceremony on the 21 April 1963, to enable work to begin on the new Bethany Baptist church in Heol Llanishen Fach. Revd Gwynfryn Thomas, at the same time, indicates the space where the communion table will be situated while one of the trustees looks on. Gwynfryn was a much loved pastor of Bethany who took the church through this early period of its development.

Opposite below: Bethany Lifeboys, in around 1967 with their leaders. Included in the photograph are: Denis Read, Christine Lewis, Revd Gwynfryn Thomas, Enid Jennings and Howard Thomas.

The cast of *Queen Elizabeth Slept Here* in a Rhiwbina Amateur Theatrical Society production from November 1958.

The cast included: Clifford Marshall, Joan Rudge, Alun Jones, Maura Donovan, David Elliot, Pamela Crossling, Margaret England, Brian Evans, Moira Brown, Jean Kent, Christine Evans, Wallis Barkway and Stan Corlett.

Rhiwbina Amateur Theatrical Society – RATS to the locals – first took to the boards in February 1958 with their first production, *The Hollow*, by Agatha Christie.

The society was formed in 1957 when the officers were Chairman, Mr Wallis Barkway, Treasurer Mr D. Elliot and Secretary Mrs J. Kent.

The cast of the play *The House by the Lake*, performed by RATS in January 1960. A newspaper comment at the time reported that the company 'were fortunate having Julia Hitchings in the leading role, portrayed with sensitivity and skill.' Apparently after the performance snow fell heavily outside and ice cream circulated freely on the stage. Current members might remark on how things have changed!

Members of the Rhiwbina Townswomen's Guild recalling a century of women.

Members of Rhiwbina Townswomen's Guild; a young Alison Fear, (*née* Cowley), is pictured third from the right.

The combined choirs of All Saints, Beulah, Bethany and Ararat performing *Messiah* at the Monico cinema. The conductor was Mike Thomas of Bethany. The front seats had to be removed to accommodate the orchestra.

The platform party at the official opening of Llanishen Fach county primary school on 15 June 1965. The speaker is County Councillor D. Arthur Thomas, who opened the school; the commemorative plaque was unveiled by Mrs Thomas, seated to his left, and the prayer of dedication was led by Revd T. Glyndwr Jones the Minister of Beulah.

Rhiwbina's camera club at one of its exhibitions in 1971. From left to right are: Jim Yendle, Stan Williams and Eric Taylor. The club originates from 1958 when it was known as the Rhiwbina Photographic Society and met in the memorial hall. When Rhiwbina's library opened in 1960, the society rented the lecture room at a cost of 15s for a two-hour session. In 1969, it changed its title to the Rhiwbina Camera Club and now meets regularly in Canolfan Beulah. The club is always looking for new members.

The new Rhiwbina school in Heol Ucha in 1928.

A view of the Deri looking south east in the early 1950s. Note the Deri Farm (now the Deri Inn) which was situated behind the large trees on the right. Also note that the new housing development on Llanishen Fach had not yet taken place.

The Deri Shop was a grocery store for several years. It was owned by the Bartley family during which time it also housed a café at the rear.

Rhiwbina's brook, attractively running through Pen-y-dre with Beulah Chapel in the background.

A unique day in the life of Rhiwbina; the village came to a halt after a heavy snow storm in 1983. A queue is forming to collect milk, and there is no other traffic – how wonderful!

Llanishen Fach school choir in the 1960s assembled for an official opening of the school.

The Victorian toilet behind Beulah Chapel before its demolition in the early 1990s. France may have its *Clochemerle* (the 1947 Chevallier film in which a progressive mayor of a small conservative French village decides to build a public convenience in the town square much to the horror of its inhabitants) but Rhiwbina now has its 'Super Loo'.

This event prompted John Rhys, a local resident, to write this whimsical piece, *Three of the People's Councillors.*

Three of the People's Councillors
Counsel together took
To build a People's Wonderloo
Above Rhiwbina Brook.

They chose the perfect setting
For this great amenity
Beside historic Beulah Church,
Where everyone could see.

'To match this fair environment',
They said, 'and do it well,
We'll summon out of Disneyland
The Architect from Hell'.

The Council team one morning
Arrived, all wreathed in smiles,
Bringing with the blueprints
Grey lavatorial tiles.

They followed the instructions
With ever widening grin,
Sticking those lavatorial tiles

With a painted plastic dome
Completing the enhancement
Of this little home from home,
They raised its humble profile

The good Rhiwbina people
Will need the proper coins
To enter the pagoda
And relieve their bursting loins.

To exit after flushing
They'll have to get away
In five and forty seconds flat
To miss the interior spray.

So the Rhiwbina Village folk
With deep emotion shook
To see the pale grey Wonderloo
Haunting Rhiwbina Brook.

We use this piece here, with permission, so that we can end on an amusing note, and look forward with hope to what is yet to be in the Rhiwbina village story.

Other local titles published by Tempus

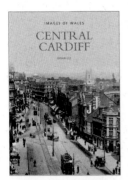

Central Cardiff
BRIAN LEE

With over 200 photographs this book conducts the reader on a tour of this most historic of cities, which has vastly changed over the years. The reader will encounter historic buildings including Cardiff Castle and the Empire Games swimming pool, knocked down to make way for the Millennium Stadium, which replaced the famous Cardiff Arms Park, as well as street scenes from the last 100 years showing pubs, cinemas, and shops that are long gone.

07524 1138 1

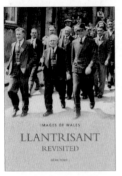

Llantrisant Revisited
DEAN POWELL

This collection of over 200 old images pays tribute to the people who have proudly called Llantrisant their home. With in-depth text, the reader is taken on a journey through the town, stopping at the High Street and Southgate, and meeting memorable individuals. *Llantrisant Revisited* offers a nostalgic and valuable record of the past, and will provide newcomers with an understanding of how the modern community of the area has evolved.

07524 3216 8

Cardiff Rugby Football Club 1940-2000
ALAN EVANS AND DUNCAN GARDINER

The rich history of Cardiff Rugby Football Club is vividly brought to life in this superb book. Over sixty years of history is covered, including the time a bomb fell on Cardiff Arms Park in 1941, victories over the All Blacks and Wallabies, the centenary year, some astonishing cup wins during the 1980s and the pursuit of glory in Europe in recent times.

07524 2181 6

Mid-Rhondda: From Penygraig to Llwynypia
DAVID J. CARPENTER

Once a sparsely-populated area, the Rhondda Valley became heavily industrialised with the arrival of coal mining. Some 150 years later, however, the mines are closed and the recession has stolen away the livelihoods of many. A fighting spirit in hard times is now remembered, as a brighter, greener future approaches. With over 180 archive images this pictorial history charts the rise and fall of the industrial societies of Tonypandy, Penygraig, Trealaw, Clydach Vale and Llwynypia.

07524 3210 9

If you are interested in purchasing other books published by Tempus, or in case you have difficulty finding any Tempus books in your local bookshop, you can also place orders directly through our website

www.tempus-publishing.com